Light Turnout

poems by

Gary Percesepe

Finishing Line Press
Georgetown, Kentucky

Light Turnout

Copyright © 2021 by Gary Percesepe
ISBN 978-1-64662-709-7 First Edition
All rights reserved under International and Pan-American Copyright Conventions. No part of this book may be reproduced in any manner whatsoever without written permission from the publisher, except in the case of brief quotations embodied in critical articles and reviews.

ACKNOWLEDGMENTS

Names, characters, places, and incidents either are products of the author's imagination or are used fictitiously. Any resemblance to actual events or persons, living or dead, is entirely coincidental.

A number of these stories appeared in slightly different form elsewhere, and in some cases titles and names of characters have been changed.

The author wishes to thank the following publications, where many of these poems and stories first appeared in print or online:

Another Crisis, Philosophy, Situation Room, and The Bench in New World Writing
Neighbors in *The Greensboro Review*
Dead Poets, Emergency, Report, and Dada in *UCity Review*
Relations in *Westchester Review*
Some Angels in *Prometheus Dreaming*
What Henry Thought in *Bull Fiction*
Here, Conversation, and New Year in *FRiGG*
Youth in *The Maine Review*
Lost Father, Shame, Light Turnout, Captain Ahab Surveys the Damage at the Press Conference, and Resurrection in *New World Writing*

Special thanks to my family, especially Jae & Vinny. I love you both, immeasurably.

To Ashton: I hope this book amuses you.

Finally, to Resea: my heart.

Publisher: Leah Huete de Maines
Editor: Christen Kincaid
Cover Art: Pier Rodolon
Author Photo: Resea Burns
Cover Design: Elizabeth Maines McCleavy

Order online: www.finishinglinepress.com
also available on amazon.com

Author inquiries and mail orders:
Finishing Line Press
PO Box 1626
Georgetown, Kentucky 40324
USA

Table of Contents

Another Crisis 1

Philosophy 2

Situation Room 3

Neighbors 4

The Best Seller 5

Report 6

The Bench 7

Emergency 8

Here 9

Liturgy of the Hours 10

Some Angels 11

Dead Poets 12

Memory Palace 13

What Henry Thought 14

Dada 15

Relations 16

The Year in Review 17

Youth 18

Conversation 20

New Year 21

Lost Father 22

Shame 23

Light Turnout 24

Captain Ahab Surveys the Damage at the Press Conference 25

Resurrection 26

For Jae & Vinny, Resea & Ashton

Another Crisis

Lester was lamenting the state of things we'd gotten ourselves into. "We've missed too many boats." I could see his brain working overtime in there, like his skull was full of panting egrets. He worried about anything, like the recent hole in Canada. This was how life had become. "You know something," Lester said, "I don't care," moving his lips like the wings of a small butterfly. "Let's face it, in times like these it's worth uncorking a case of blips from the archives". We shared a good meal, Lester and me, slurping from the milk pail. Lester grabbed from the newer vegetables. "What's another crisis, we've seen worse." He looked over at his mother, who sagged sideways in a wheelchair. A crowd gathered in the lobby. Every face looked like a dinner guest sketched on the gaslit air. A downed tree would have put it better.

Philosophy

Everyone was talking about a philosophy of life. It seemed important and the kind of thing that could stand one in good stead for years to come. Things were falling apart. The ex: money again. No news there. My best friend Flipper was freaking out on me again. Two kids in need of school clothes and new footwear. And I had a brother in rehab. Then the dog died. I swear, I couldn't believe what was happening. Every time I turned around, atomic. The kids made me write a funeral service. We threw the goldfish in the hole; yep, they came up dead too. I needed to get ready for an important job interview but had nothing to wear. Flipper offered his suit, which was a kind but stupid gesture, since he is a 52 long. Are you with me here? The sky stretched thin and pale, loaded with cumulous. I couldn't notice, I was up to my neck. I told Flipper that if I couldn't write it up I wouldn't know what has happening to me? I said it just like that with a question mark at the end? You know? The way I learned from my ex, who learned from Oprah? And he laughed and passed gas and told me to forget about it. And I said, I am serious, I do not know what I am thinking until I write it out. And he goes, that is one scary mothafucker. Which I had to agree with. Right here was when I caught my mother screwing some man in her apartment. I walked in with her Chiclets and she was on the couch putting out for this guy, he looked like Marv Albert. With the hair piece, the big voice! SPREEWELL IS ON FIRE! The guy from 1050 ESPN radio who calls the Knicks games is screwing my mom for all he's worth, and she's holding on for dear life. All I could do was look. It was like my own private Sopranos episode. Her dentures popping. Oh God, it is so disgusting. They're going at it like a pair of pit bulls and Flipper comes over from next door to see what is the racket? When he sees, he leaves the room like it's the most normal thing of the week, he nonchalants it. I am glued to the floor. Neither of them notice me. My mom's hearing aid is loose and flapping. SPREEWELL AT THE TOP OF THE KEY, CIRCUS SHOT! Flipper returns carrying a fire extinguisher. I tell him, my heart. I'd like to die. Marv is covered in white. He has a stripe on his back from the foam on his black T, and let's face it, he looks like an angry Pepé Le Pew. I hand him a towel, nod at mother. My mother! for chrissake. Later I wrote my mother a strongly worded letter. She never believed a word of it.

Situation Room

Two men in blue serge suits sat roasting at the station. Overhead, an enormous fan turned slowly beneath a constellated sky. Edgar was newly retired from the physics department at the New School. He smoked a briarwood pipe and blew smoke rings through the air, obsessed with a new geometry supple enough to spread malaise evenly through the universe. Brother Allyoop surveyed the passing crowd, pausing to admire portraits of presidents mounted in the Beaux Arts lobby. People and luggage moved swiftly through the station, with the occasional dog. A needle-nosed man in a stovepipe hat gestured up at Orion's belt and remarked, This is America! Content with a progressive tax code and cars with chrome wings, each citizen a locker room of numbskull ideas like perfume in a toothpaste cap. Edgar nodded at the topper and worked his math. Mayonnaise spread like the silent prayer of a Buddhist. From Alleyoop not a bang nor a whimper, more a slow leak of fluid. Alleyoop saluted the stiffening substance dripping from the door hinge of the stationmaster. His cell phone buzzed. It was the president, wanting to speak with Edgar. Have you noticed the mayo, the president said. Edgar allowed as how, well, yes he had. Just act like nothing's going on, the president said. Edgar handed me the phone. The president repeated, Nothing is happening, you see? Yes, Mr. President, I said. My tongue was flecked with mayo. It roamed north of my lips, and I extended my tongue to capture what I could while holding the phone to my head and nodding to Edgar. The sun travels all day then falls down, Alleyoop whispered in my wet ear. I won't let on, I told the president, even if they torture me. I immediately regretted the word torture, but it was too late for a quick edit. Edgar giggled. A crowd gathered. Allyoop stood to his feet, applauding. Someone started singing Elvira. Edgar supplied the *oom poppa, oom poppa,* banging his pipe on his shoe. The sudden pressure to act normal never seemed harder. I thought fondly of my washer, a Kenmore newly installed in my basement, beside the dryer. Both of them sporting normal buttons. That helped. We will get through this, I said to the phone.

Neighbors

The neighbor next door lugged a giant eraser into the yard and called for his son, Ben. Ted worked methodically, beginning with Ben's unfortunate lime flip-flops, and moving rapidly toward the torso.

Ted! I called, jumping the low fence. Just then, Ted's wife barged out the back door carrying mint juleps. Ted, what are you doing? I asked.

I'm erasing my son, Ted said.

And this is OK with you? I asked Mary.

Is what OK?

Erasing your son, I said. She shrugged her shoulders and gulped her mint julep. He was a mistake, she said.

Even so, I said.

Ben was almost gone. A mouth, a flash of eyebrow, a mop of reddish hair. It's not fair, he started to say, but Ted made a few quick swipes and there was only a red smudge in the grass.

My turn, Mary said. She aimed the eraser at Ted's ample ass, using both hands.
Hey, I said, wanting to help but not knowing how, exactly.

What about the lawn mower? I finally said.

What about it, Mary said. She stopped to finish her drink. Her pretty face was a fine menace.

Can I have it? The lawnmower, I mean. And maybe some gas?

Sure, she said. Help yourself. Enjoy it while you can.

The Best Seller

I was at the Super Bowl. It was one week before the big game. I took myself out to the parking lot, to have a smoke. The TV guys were there, row after row of trucks with satellite antennas high on the roof as far as eye could see. A matte black armored car driving at a high rate of speed crashed through the gate. I understood that this was a terrorist attack--within minutes, the gate would be repaired by a crew that would later emerge, and the terrorists would embed with journalists, waiting for just the right moment to blow up the Super Bowl and have it televised, live. I thought about telling Resea, but what would I say? I was now a material witness to an act of terror. The FBI was out of the question. The thing to do was to write a novel, quickly, Tom Clancy style, before the big game, then get it instantly published and cash in. I composed the novel in my head, each line magically appearing in a long procession of sentences. It was thrilling. But I started to get hung up on the technical stuff, the electronics of it all, how the terrorists would trigger this and that and rewire and jigger things--who knows how that works? Likewise, the cops who were in on it, the inner FBI workings, who has time to keep up on all the conspiracies? Plus, I'd have to pay consultants to learn all this stuff, to get it word perfect, and some asshole would still criticize the work, a whole industry of people spotting plot holes and worse, I'd have to share the money with them and with all the lawyers. My book was a royal pain in the ass. I was sick and tired of it. I started to curse and get into a nasty mood. It was all over for me. Done. Baked. I was a loser, had it tattooed on my forehead. Sloppily. Looked like some dime-store rub on. Just a stink on me. Then I realized: I do not have to write this book. No one knows. I am alone with my secrets. They are so lovely.

Report

A dispute broke out at the edge of the property line, rattling the eggs in the pantry causing misfires on the frying pans. It erupted into a war in no time at all, then fell back into disputed territory, and stopped altogether. Someone proposed plastering the windows with wood pulp as protection against the noonday enigmas, others formed a resistance. Each new investigation rebuilt the urgency like a sand rampart until we all fell asleep. Further reflection undermined it, causing its eventual collapse. What was strange was that we could see the dispute as a curving abacus in full urgency mode from Day One, but by then dispatches hardly mattered. Camaraderie, or something like it, pored over us like covfefe. There was a general search for one correct attitude. Nights arrived like a friendly takeover.

The Bench

Everything could have been different, yet all remains the same. For years Batgirl circled the globe, her eyes puddled with tears. Euripides, I'm told, despite his fame, clipped toenails in solitude. What I mean to say is, be patient with me, I'm lolling on the banks of a thought. I waited while she applied moisturizer to her legs. She resembled in those days a lake of gravy into which I was prone to dive, inadvisably. You smell like my subconscious, she once offered. Are you talking to me? I asked. Don't be silly, she said. A squirrel tottered on the squirrel highway. Why are squirrels always doing that, she asked. Doing what, I asked. Always jerking around, like their heads are soldered with bad wire. Oh, I said. A cop came up to us. Do you have a permit to sit on this bench, he asked. Why no, officer, she said. That's OK, the cop said, we no longer require a permit. I pulled my hands off the bench, where I'd been tapping out a Norwegian melody. What did you do, she asked the cop. Nothing, he said, I was off duty. He sighed. I began to tap again. You have a fragility a wife could work with, she said. We both turned and asked, Me? Children are the most interesting to talk to, she said. They tell you what they know, then they stop.

Emergency

This is how my days & nights pass in a crowded apartment of ideas overlooking last week's sinkhole. The weather remains unthinkable. Urchins race up and down the avenue. My friend Skip languished in a nearby hospital. My bunions are in an uproar! he'd tease. Moments before his death he was chipper enough to bemoan the cheese on the burger. How do people live like this? I hate these passing days & keep imagining another may happen by to fall in love with. Like a wizard with a new wand. Meanwhile, the government made policy by picture puzzle. Moonflowers shimmered in the street dust. All the pieces fit but the frame had disappeared.
Outside my window, a man carried a sofa. In the light of the streetlamp the stranger grew stranger.

Here

Resea tells me about the doctor she works with at Memorial Sloane Kettering Cancer Center. Wednesday is the day Dr. Francis removes the eyes of babies, Resea says. I'm not sure I heard that right. We're stopped at a traffic light close to the White Plains train station. Baby eyes? From cancer, yes. How do the parents know, I ask? Resea says what usually happens is the parents take their baby for their first picture portrait, and the photographer notices a milky film behind the pupil; when light hits the eye, it looks white or black instead of red. They take the baby to an eye doctor, where they get the news. Then, it's MSK. The eye is removed. If it's both eyes they remove the worst one, then do radiation on the second. We are at the station. She leans over to kiss me and is out the door, wearing the animal print leggings I got her in Paris, and a cutaway black coat that I love. Her hair is longer now; the purple ends rest lightly on the black coat as she walks quickly to meet her train to Manhattan. For three years she has been cancer-free. It is the day that the president will be impeached by Congress. We had an ice storm two days ago, and the trees are painted silver and black. In our back yard, the branches of the cherry tree hang almost to the ground. I look for the red cardinal who is a regular, nod when I see him, and try to think about dinner. I decide I will make pasta, which means Balducci's in Scarsdale to get what I need, with some white birch for the fireplace. We will stay in tonight. I will grab a bottle of champagne from the wine store across from Balducci's. Maybe Resea can just take the train from Grand Central to the Scarsdale station? I can pick her up there. The babies, I think. I'm looking up at the sky as I drive up my street, lined with fairy tale Tudors, copper guttering glinting through the sun. Your baby's eye is going to be removed, today. I think of the parents. In the room, waiting. The president will be impeached. We will drink our champagne by the fire. Whatever happens today, we are here.

Liturgy of the Hours

Sometimes late at night my dead sister visits and it is always the same, where the forest runs down to the sea I lie in bed and listen for the murmur of the ocean, the great soft sound of it, until it seems my mother sings a low soft lullaby; though I live alone we are all present, my father sitting by the fireplace mending his torn sweater, the four of us safely gathered, my brother still nine, the year of his departure, my sister six, while my four year old self drifts to sleep dreaming of the meadow that runs to the foaming sea, blue with flowers. When I wake there is no one to tell the dream until moonlight lies again on the floor like the white skin of my sister and I begin again to speak of the seal rocks on the coast hidden in shadow, and the mermaid whose song is heard just beyond the last white line of the waves, appears-- her showery head bobbing in the silvery night, her voice like running water, and I forget that I had ever lived alone.

Some Angels

Some angels broke into my bedroom. Soldiers of the lord they called themselves. They spirited me off in my sleep, brutal wings flapping.

We landed on the roof of the house. They tossed shingles, calling them the pages of my life. The book of the roof, they cracked. From the roof we could see the shattered hulk of an abandoned ship, its hull barnacled and bleeding.

My sister and brother appeared, long dead beside my mother and father. We were led away, one by one in single file past the stairways of our beds. Deeper into our dreams, which clutched us like tree roots. In slow surrender, we tossed and turned through decades of damp night.

The dead swam in the dark. Suspension bridges built without pilings spanned the open sea, bobbing like corks in the ocean, bridge after bridge, complex strands of steel cables singing in the wind like giant harps, trafficless and stunning in their beauty. One angel gripped my forearm. Everything is made of time, even these clouds, he said. They merge and tear and pull away at last.

Dead Poets
> *The world is ugly*
> *And the people are sad* ~ Wallace Stevens

The night was filled with voices and signals. Roads not taken reappeared. Driving past the anniversary of my death I passed a chipmunk taking a dump in tall fescue by the side of the road. This wasn't morning, it was a dream of morning, I thought, slapping my forehead. Dogs to decades, my half-life's as crumbling infrastructure to her! Breakfast was wild, she later observed, R rated thanks to the neighbor who ankled over. It's only yesterday but already seems to be the middle of next week. I remembered the neighbor. She lost her husband during the divorce. It was cold in the big house. Pipes blinked open and poured out gravy. Great, I thought, the rest is gravy. Basement life seemed to suit the neighbor. You're a gleam of sun on fresh snow, I wanted to say. Sawdust piled up around my best intentions. Night found Socrates buzzed but not drunk, I recalled from the *Symposium*, alone under the ponderous stars. His head splintered by a thousand thoughts.

Memory Palace

The house was solitary and dark. I walked around back and tried the door. It was locked. Black rotted vines covered the crumbling brick walls. The vines pulled off in my hand, useless for climbing. The moon peaked out from behind a cloud, illuminating a fire escape. I climbed to the landing on the top floor where I encountered a man named Steve. He was just leaving, he said, but I was welcome to join him. "What's inside," I asked. "It's a memory palace," Steve said. "What's that," I asked. "You're here for Jennifer," he said, "aren't you?" "How did you know," I asked. "Everyone comes by here looking," he said. This seemed implausible. I knew several people, maybe dozens of people, who didn't know Jennifer. I told Steve this. "Nonsense," he said. "We've been waiting for you." We entered the big living room. The room was littered with old records, 45s and 8 tracks and CDs, comic books, baseball cards. A pile of fringed cowboy clothes rested on a winged backed chair, all sizes. Batons and whistles, cheerleader uniforms with matching underwear, sports bras, boots and shoes, tie dyed T-shirts, and loads of costume jewelry. There were children's books and coloring books and brightly colored sticker books and glitter makeup, but everything seemed to belong to the same childhood. The bath toys looked lonely on the living room floor, holding traces of the children from whom they'd departed. I felt Jennifer's familiar gaze coming from a painting on the wall but when I mentioned this to Steve he laughed. "Look again." he said. I looked and there were no paintings on any of the walls. "What you feel looking at you is from the Jennifer you brought here. You're responsible. In the Memory Palace nothing is ever lost, everything is just misplaced." I went to the window and looked down at the ruined French garden. An old man in a police uniform was there to arrest me. "But officer," I said, "I'm an old man." "And yet this is your first visit," he said. Steve brought us cups of tea served from Jennifer's silver tea service. We sat in the garden drinking. Jennifer waved from the wide window.

What Henry Thought

Henry wanted to scream but the TV people said it wouldn't matter. But Henry felt better today. He had a chirp when he walked and a smoky little kitchen garden, some rabbits in the dispensary. I miss the days of wine and roses, he said to himself. But yonder, where stars once grew for me, the sky looks threatening. Better to tend this kitchen garden. He checked the freezer. One fallen ice cube was left, like your conscience after a hangover. We know these women by our post cards, Harry thought, beautiful but inclined to blow away. The days tumble over us. Outside, water rained on water. Land stretched like jelly to the farthest cliff. When I was young I could smell the loam rise like a scented caress. A hummingbird performed with silver sound. Henry imagined himself sitting by the pier next to the fjord. We'll stay clean, by God, he said. When the facts reach us, we'll yelp and admit no mistakes.

Dada

Much later I'd wonder about St. Louis and how it kept me as a place holder for something else, for instance the woman who sat across the red banquette in the Chase Plaza Hotel with her friend, who laughed at my jokes, received my film review with amusement and left with her friend just when things might have been otherwise, and the way, for me, this always triggers a memory of my father standing unsteadily on two war-damaged legs, how he failed to cradle my head warm to his chest but left to fell forests and wrote no letters but held a lantern high when we walked out into the night. When she left, I stood out in a thunderstorm hoping to be hit by lightning, but it missed, first left, then right, and my father's voice saying, she's slender and strange, the way you like. As my father grows in me, I cede more and more territory and accept our defeats.

Relations

We were survivors of a dead mother and no-account father. A stink was on us. We accepted the fact. We had one true friend, Old Bill. He had known our mother, but only when she was hiding out from our father, if you follow. Old Bill always told us the same story about Mom fainting when we was born. He'd cross his knobby knees and spit in the spittoon, and say, Now boys, it wasn't just when you was born that your Mama fainted. She fainted from the slightest thing that stirred her. We didn't really want to hear about that, again, so we always turned up the Farm Report on the radio. Pork bellies swung from the rafters. But Old Bill would be rolling like a hog truck on a gravel road going straight downhill. He was not a man to dip his donut, is what he said. Said he was a stallion of misbehavior. We wanted to shoot out his stoplight, but he was family, you see. This man to be reckoned with, our manly mentor. Old Bill had lived on nothing but crayfish for seven years, it was rumored. Boys, Old Bill said, Your mother would say to me, what say we unzip Old Trigger there, and let him out of the barn. And he went on in this general vein.

The Year in Review

I sat at my desk and made a list of all my accomplishments this year. I won the hot dog contest at Nathan's in Coney Island! Well, not exactly. I'd backed out at the last minute, forfeiting the entrance fee. The thought of dipping hot dog buns into a jar of water to make things go faster repulsed me. A wet soggy hot dog bun? No thanks. But I had caught the biggest Bluefin tuna on record in Montauk. Also, false. I set a new land speed record on the Taconic Parkway in my new Porsche. Nope. I sat and dozed at the desk. A mouse awakened me, nibbling the toes of my left foot. I threw the book of psalms at him and he scampered off into his hole in the wall. I'd won the home beautification award in Westchester for the third consecutive year! Fat chance. What about the three days in a row I called in sick at the office while I lazed in Aruba? That felt like a triumph. And I had kited a check successfully with hours to spare before my paycheck was automatically deposited, avoiding tons of fees. There was the best seller I'd authored in my head, which I'd wisely avoided writing once I figured out the mess in taxes I'd face, not to mention doing the obligatory book tour, having to face all those annoying literary lions with their cloying introductions, and sycophantic MFA students asking countless questions about my "process." Process my ass, I told them, in the dream that accompanied my heroic decision to forego writing the novel. I looked down the page, at my mounting successes. A baseball shattered the window. Glass was all over my desk. It was the doofus kid from next door, Timmy or Tommy, or whatever his name was. I invited him in, swept away the broken glass, sat him down at my desk, brought him a hot dog and shot of scotch. He politely declined. "I'm ten years old," he said. I complimented him on his restraint, and downed the scotch, saving the hot dog for later. All the while complimenting him on his good sense about liquor, which had led to the downfall of many a good man, and reflected well, I thought, on his parents. I told Timmy this. Or Tommy. "Can I have my ball back, mister?" he asked. I gave him his damn ball and added this to my burgeoning list. I was rolling, now.

Youth

I ran away with a girl one summer. We stole money from our parents and stuffed our things into a large backpack. Jacqueline had two pairs of jeans, a thin leather jacket, bras, her pairs of red espadrilles, assorted oversized sweaters, and toiletries. I put some shirts, pants, and underwear in the backpack with a couple of first editions from my father's library that I hoped to sell.

We made it to London where it rained for two weeks. Our room was close to the train station. The room had a sickly-sweet smell that clung to our clothes and seemed embedded in the pores of our skin. The smell must have come from the drain, or the nearby kitchen, or the rotting green carpet. Each morning we went for long walks in Hyde Park to escape the smell, but the rain would drive us into department stores or movie theatres, where we watched looping newsreels and the feature movie. It didn't matter that the same movie repeated night after night.

One afternoon in the London Underground, at the Charing Cross station we had our pictures taken in a PhotoMat. We posed with our faces close together. I kept the picture as a souvenir. Jacqueline's face is in the foreground, and mine is set back slightly, cut off by the edge of the photo, so that my right ear is missing.

The money we had stolen didn't go far and the first editions brought a pittance. At night we teamed up to pick the pockets of tourists in Trafalgar Square. Jacqueline got a job cleaning an office building. She went through the trash looking for anything that would help us make money. We were able to blackmail some poor bastard who had stupidly thrown into the trash a letter from his mistress.

In a public house not far from the international youth hostel on Oxford Street, a man sat down at our table without saying hello. He was of average height and quite fat, round face, bald in front and on top, and he wore tortoise shell glasses. His childlike hands contrasted with his substantial build. A cigarette dangled from his mouth and ash had dropped onto the lapels of his tweed jacket. He said his name was Renchfort. He had heard about our predicament and wanted to help. I knew he was lying, as we had no friends who would tell him such a thing. I told him to go to hell. He insisted that he meant no harm, and that he wanted only to be of service. He swallowed his smile when I called him a pervert and told him to try a different hostel. But Jacqueline pulled his unlit cigarette from his mouth and asked him for a light. He slid a thin blue envelope across the small table. Jacqueline took the envelope and excused herself. In the bathroom she opened the envelope and found a 100£ bank note and an address, written in a shaky hand. Jacqueline returned from the loo. She swept the ash from Renchfort's lapels and slapped his face. No, she said. Not there. We would return to our hotel room which smelled of rotten carpet and filthy water, or not at all. I was paid an additional 100£ to watch.

After the PhotoMat flashed our picture that afternoon in the London Underground we couldn't stop laughing, and Jacqueline wanted to stay seated on my knees for a long time. Much later, I found the picture in an old suitcase of letters, and I was struck by the innocence of our faces. We inspired trust in people. We had no real qualities, except for the one youth gives to everyone for a brief time, like a vague promise that will never come true.

Conversation

My girlfriend talked like one of the sea people, her voice salt and water, a queer liquid laugh. She'd peek over my shoulder and say: Another poem that's not about me. Most of us occupy the wrong space in the human parking lot, I'd reply. Alone among the animals we babysit ourselves listening to the shrill music of adolescence of which the less said, the better. I sat on the toilet in the lobby bathroom at the Waldorf Astoria for several hours hiding from her. She came from a small town in Illinois where most of the residents were under house arrest, having misplaced their sliver of luck. I tipped the attendant and strolled outside. Thoughts coursed through my head like scampering mice. In our dreams the poet says we stand on shore for what seems an eternity and it is always the wrong shore.

New Year

It was a season of losses. Next to go was that evening's asparagus cluster. Before they could be sautéd, they launched and lodged in an Encyclopedia Britannia. Blinkered trail horses bolted the bridge to New Jersey, the Mayor in hot pursuit. Then, everything went still for a minute. Even the mice in the kitchen quit foraging, settling old debts. The New Year had arrived, swaddled like a baby. Grain will ripen, I thought. Oaks will blossom. Rivers still run from the mountains to the sea. The doorbell rang. It was my portly neighbor Rob. I kissed him and said wait here. I told Rob that it was true, what the poet said, that you can feel happy with one piece of your heart. I went to fetch those shelved asparagus, tearful in Volume N.

Lost Father

I'd read somewhere that at certain hours of the night you can slip into a parallel world: an empty apartment where the light wasn't switched off, on a dead-end street. It's where one finds objects lost long ago: a lucky charm, a letter, an umbrella, a key. A dog that followed me through the streets of Paris. The dog walked in front of me. At first, it looked around to check that I was following, and then it walked at a steady pace, certain that I would follow. I walked at the same slow pace as the dog. Nothing interrupted the silence. Grass seemed to grow in between the cobblestones. Time had ceased. Facades of buildings, the trees, the glimmer of the streetlamps took on an intensity that I had never seen in them before.

The entrance halls of certain buildings retain the echo of footsteps of those who used to cross them and who have since vanished. Something continues to vibrate after they have gone, fading waves, but which can still be picked up if one listens.

I thought of my father. I imagined him in that room on the dead-end street, or in a café just before closing time, sitting alone under the neon lights, looking through his files. He is working late. There is still a chance that I will find him.

Shame

It is the hour at last to replace my face. The architecture here is far from reassuring. Every night we tally the dead, but no one is ever missing. I sat in bed and tried to write this poem. The puppy nipped at my hand which hung over the side of the bed. I tried some sentences, but nothing seemed to work the way it should. Imagine me pregnant and in profile and it'll explain the president. He is the bee in the mattress. My calendar is in order. My clothes closet is ship shape. I licked blood from my finger and thought things like, Would I recognize my obituary? I felt I wanted to creep into an arctic cave to check the rectal temperature of the biggest bear. Then the puppy yelped and looked at me with his sad ten-week eyes, and I felt the fog lift from the soup bowl. I thought of all those never famous men. Fame makes you lazy. All you know is ears. All wars are useless to the dead. That's when I realized my granny called me Flapdoodle and I don't know two specks about what's coming next. Why worry? The dog looked at me, head tilted, as if to say we are all carved from the same carrot. Should I go on? Aimee & Valerie hotted up my inbox which otherwise was dignified and stale. I thought of all my old lovers, how fine they were now. Finally sorted out, a happy thought for each. Goodbye, girls, goodbye! All my best thoughts limp after you.

Light Turnout

Something in the dirty salad of lies stuck in my throat. I felt that dread of the future peculiar to mothers. I shut down the engine, then thought better of it and took a drive through the prairie. New revelations awaited. One more mile could save my life, then another. It was easier this way. There was the world's largest spool of thread, and across the street, a woman who lived in a shoe, complete with giftshop and tavern. I pulled in and shared a beer with a local citizen named Birdie who told me he'd relocated his mind once he untangled his parachute. This seemed more than a metaphor. He leaned over to kiss me. I ducked and paid my bill. Exiting, I saw some tangled trees that looked like seaweed in the twilight. Clouds were shifting to purple and a cool breeze blew my hat down the road. I saw then that Birdie had followed me out. He had my hat. "What people forget about her," he said, gesturing at the old woman in the shoe who towered over the roadside, "was how she whipped all them kids and put 'em all to bed." "Thank you," I said, accepting the hat. "No broth, either," I added, but he wasn't tracking. Instead, he grabbed me by the shoulders and turned me back around. "You feel the need that almost everyone in a defeated country must feel," he said.

Captain Ahab Surveys the Damage at the Press Conference

The women in the back wore dead smiles. They all had the superior look of people out of work. A sign hung in the hallway said, "No suicides permitted here." Heavy hearted cheers arose from the gem colored polos in the front. Ahab mounted the podium like fate into the lone Atlantic. He spoke at length of the permitting stars which weave round them tragic graces. Reporters glared back, crucifixion in their eyes. Ahab's face was a pale half-a-loaf face. "Avast!" he cried. "Sing out for new stars." "Will you be requiring all Americans to wear masks, sir?" someone asked. "Mask, flask," stormed the Captain. Then was heard a terrific, loud, animal sob like that of a heart-stricken moose. It was the Attorney General, hot as Satan's hoof. "Stand by me," Starbuck prayed, his Quaker voice a tremble. "Hold me, blind me, O ye blessed influences!" Ahab rowed on into the wind. Snowflakes tumbled in feathery confusion, wonderfully white against the night, smothering the whole dirty, roaring, guilty city in innocence and silence. Like the unabated Hudson when that noble Northman flows narrowly but unfathomingly through Poughkeepsie. The virus was alluded to, never mentioned. But it was the whiteness of the thing that above all appalled, said Flask. "This whiteness," said the third mate, "keeps her ruins for ever-new." "Flask, Flask," roared Ahab. "Flask is a butterless man."

Resurrection
> *We are born, buried for a while, then spring up just as everything is closing* ~ John Ashbery

Judges marched backwards up the steps. I saw it was time to question the trees. Now all the leaves lie brown in the ditch. Girls gone. The newly shoed horses fled the barn in disgust. The road, or is it roadbed, winds into a new landscape and runs away with us while our mood tries its best to stay fixed.

All we need to do is stay. It's easy to get lost, like a penis caught in a zipper. Turn a blind eye, sure, all of that. I had forgotten what a bird looked like. My thoughts kept wandering down to the river to have a look.

I began to think that only death cancels all our engagements. I thought: You came here in a fucking Ford. Now what?

From here I could hear the sad bells of other hometowns. My tires had spat out miles like spools of thread. Just one drop of atheism lasts a long time in this landscape.

Clouds were banked and stacked, each jockeying for the top position before sliding back again, as if moved by sun rays, each promised to a bridesmaid. I felt again I had been returned to the nominative case.

We always stay the same, and the people we have been in the past whiz by until the end of time.

Gary Percesepe is the author of eleven books, including MORATORIUM: COLLECTED STORIES 1995-2020. He resides in White Plains, New York, and teaches philosophy at Fordham University in the Bronx.

www.ingramcontent.com/pod-product-compliance
Lightning Source LLC
LaVergne TN
LVHW041516070426
835507LV00012B/1612